Let's Use VERBS

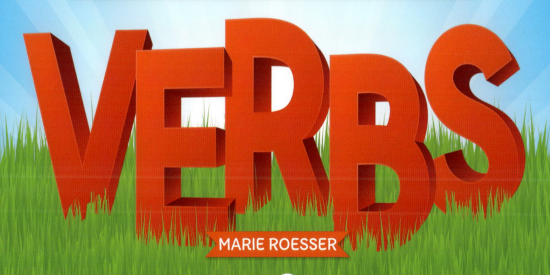

MARIE ROESSER

Please visit our website, www.enslow.com. For a free color catalog of all our high-quality books, call toll free 1-800-398-2504 or fax 1-877-980-4454.

Library of Congress Cataloging-in-Publication Data
Names: Roesser, Marie, author.
Title: Let's use verbs / Marie Roesser.
Description: New York : Enslow Publishing, [2023] | Series: Word world | Includes bibliographical references and index.
Identifiers: LCCN 2021044931 (print) | LCCN 2021044932 (ebook) | ISBN 9781978527126 (library binding) | ISBN 9781978527102 (paperback) | ISBN 9781978527119 (set) | ISBN 9781978527133 (ebook)
Subjects: LCSH: English language--Verb--Juvenile literature.
Classification: LCC PE1271 .R64 2023 (print) | LCC PE1271 (ebook) | DDC 428.2--dc23/eng/20211122
LC record available at https://lccn.loc.gov/2021044931
LC ebook record available at https://lccn.loc.gov/2021044932

Portions of this work were originally authored by Kate Mikoley and published as *Let's Learn Verbs!*. All new material this edition authored by Marie Roesser.

First Edition

Published in 2023 by
Enslow Publishing
29 E. 21st Street
New York, NY 10010

Copyright © 2023 Enslow Publishing

Designer: Katelyn Reynolds
Interior Layout: Rachel Rising
Editor: Therese Shea

Photo credits: Cover, pp. 1, 3, 4, 6, 8, 10, 12, 14, 16, 18, 20, 22–24 iadams/Shutterstock.com; Cover, p. 1 Faberr Ink/Shutterstock.com; Cover, p. 1 IIlerlok_xolms/Shutterstock.com; Cover, p. 1 LimitedFont/Shutterstock.com; p. 5 anek.soowannaphoom/Shutterstock.com; p. 7 AnnaStills/Shutterstock.com; p. 9 Syda Productions/Shutterstock.com; p. 11 LightField Studios/Shutterstock.com; p. 13 Sergey Novikov/Shutterstock.com; p. 13 mimagephotography/Shutterstock.com; p. 15 b7/Shutterstock.com; p. 17 Jaggat Rashidi/Shutterstock.com; p. 19 Monkey Business Images/Shutterstock.com; p. 21 FamVeld/Shutterstock.com.

All rights reserved. No part of this book may be reproduced in any form without permission in writing from the publisher, except by a reviewer.

Printed in the United States of America

Some of the images in this book illustrate individuals who are models. The depictions do not imply actual situations or events.

CPSIA compliance information: Batch #CSENS23: For further information contact Enslow Publishing, New York, New York, at 1-800-398-2504.

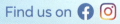

CONTENTS

Action! 4
Physical or Mental 6
Past, Present, Future 10
Irregular Verbs 16
All About Be. 18
Helping Verbs. 20
Glossary 22
Answer Key 22
For More Information 23
Index. 24

Words in the glossary appear in **bold** type the first time they are used in the text.

ACTION!

Verbs are often called action words. *Play* and *laugh* are verbs. But some verbs aren't actions. These are sometimes called being verbs. *Seem* and *be* are examples. Let's learn more! The questions in this book will help. Check your answers on page 22.

PHYSICAL OR MENTAL

Some action verbs are physical. People move their bodies to do them. Others can see these actions happening. *Swim*, *dance*, *work*, and *read* are just a few examples.

> Which of these verbs is a physical action: *hike*, *think*, or *is*?

Other kinds of verbs have to do with actions in the mind. These can be called mental verbs. You can't see them happening. *Believe, know*, and *feel* are mental verbs.

> Which mental verb fits what's happening on the next page: *learn* or *jump*?

PAST, PRESENT, FUTURE

A verb's tense tells us when the verb happened. For example, past tense verbs tell us the action already occurred. These words often end with the suffixes *-d* or *-ed*.

> Which is the past tense of the verb *kick*: *kicked* or *kicks*?

The present tense means the action is happening now. If the **subject** of the sentence is **singular**, we often add an -*s* to the verb. If the subject is **plural**, we don't add an -*s*. Read the examples on page 13.

> Which is the present tense of the verb *talk*: *talked* or *talks*?

The boy smiles.

The boys smile.

The future tense **describes** an action that hasn't happened yet but will. In fact, future tense verbs usually start with the word *will*.

Which sentence below uses the future tense of the verb *eat*?

A. Cam eats lunch.
B. Cam will eat lunch.

IRREGULAR VERBS

Many verbs don't follow common tense **patterns**. They're called irregular verbs. Think about the verb *rise*. Its past tense is *rose*, not "rised." *See*, *take*, and *throw* are also irregular verbs.

Which verb is irregular, *drive* or *move*? (Hint: Think about the past tense for each.)

ALL ABOUT BE

The verb *be* may seem tricky. *Am, is, are, was,* and *were* all come from this one verb! The subject and tense can require different verb forms.

Which form of *be* best completes the following sentences?

She was sick last night.
Now she___?___better.

SUBJECT	VERB: BE		
	past tense	present tense	future tense
I	was	am	will be
YOU	were	are	will be
HE/SHE/IT	was	is	will be
WE/YOU/THEY	were	are	will be

19

HELPING VERBS

Be is a helping verb too. *May* and *have* are two others. A helping verb comes before a main verb. It adds meaning. Let's read an example:

> I go to the zoo.
> I may go to the zoo.
>
> The helping verb *may* makes a difference! Verbs are valuable!

GLOSSARY

describe To tell what something or someone is like.
pattern A repeated way that something is done or happens.
plural A form of a word that means more than one person or thing.
singular A form of a word that means one person or thing.
subject The person, place, or thing that does the main action of a sentence.
suffix A letter or a group of letters added to the end of a word to change its meaning.

ANSWER KEY

p. 6: hike
p. 8: learn
p. 10: kicked
p. 12: talks
p. 14: B
p. 16: drive
p. 18: is

FOR MORE INFORMATION

BOOKS
Dahl, Michael. *Verbs Say "Go!"* North Mankato, MN: Picture Window Books, 2020.

Heinrichs, Ann. *Verbs*. Mankato, MN: The Child's World, 2020.

Owings, Lisa. *Chase, Wiggle, Chomp: Teaching Verbs*. Mankato, MN: The Child's World, 2017.

WEBSITES

Nouns and Verbs
www.abcya.com/nouns_and_verbs.htm
This game will help you spot both nouns and verbs.

What Are Verbs?
www.grammar-monster.com/lessons/verbs.htm
Find out much more about these words here.

Publisher's note to educators and parents: Our editors have carefully reviewed these websites to ensure that they are suitable for students. Many websites change frequently, however, and we cannot guarantee that a site's future contents will continue to meet our high standards of quality and educational value. Be advised that students should be closely supervised whenever they access the internet.

INDEX

actions, 4, 8
being verbs, 4
helping verbs, 20
irregular verbs, 16
mental verbs, 8
physical verbs, 6
plural, 12
singular, 12
subjects, 12, 18, 19
suffixes, 10
tenses, 10, 12, 14, 16, 18, 19